About the Author

Pat Long Gardner, a native of eastern Pennsylvania, lives with her husband Bill, an artist, in Sparks, Maryland.

After college Pat taught general courses in textiles to home economists, but since 1976 she has specialized in quilting at Catonsville Community College, the Maryland Institute College of Art, and at workshops from Richmond to Cape Cod.

Her studio classes draw from far and wide. Fifteen of her regular students have been meeting for more than a decade. One of them says a meeting is not a "class" but a "total immersion"— unlike typical quilt classes that concentrate on single techniques or types of design. Pat has each person working on her own projects, and each immersion begins with a show-and-tell and group critique. Beginners tend to progress more quickly, and experienced quilters gain fresh ideas from newcomers.

"I teach quilting," says Pat, "because I find a great reward in seeing people develop their own styles and confidence in creating new work." New creativity and new confidence is what **Handkerchief Quilts**, her premier book, is all about.

JED KIRSCHBAUM

For my mother,
Margaret Wiest Zug,
an avid collector of old textiles
whose interest and appreciation for quilts and handkerchiefs
sparked my own.

A special thanks to my husband Bill
for drafting the diagrams and to my daughter Rebecca for transcribing
the text and for her helpful comments.

I also appreciate the support and enthusiasm
of friends and students who embraced the idea of handkerchief quilts
and created their own one-of-a-kind treasures.

Handkerchief Quilts

Pat Long Gardner

Introduction by Carter Houck

EPM

McLean, Virginia

Library of Congress Cataloging-in-Publication Data

Gardner, Pat Long.
   Handkerchief quilts : creating unique wall hangings from
collectible handkerchiefs / Pat Long Gardner ; introduction by
Carter Houck.
      p.   cm.
   Includes bibliographical references and index.
   ISBN 0-939009-73-0
   1. Quilting—Patterns. 2. Handkerchiefs. 3. Wall hangings.
  I. Title.
TT835.G367   1993
746.3—dc20   93-10468
                                            CIP

Copyright © 1993 Pat Long Gardner
All Rights Reserved
EPM Publications, Inc., 1003 Turkey Run Road
McLean, VA 22101
Printed in the United States of America

Color Photography by Duane Suter

Cover and Book Design by Tom Huestis

Contents

Introduction

The ongoing fascination with quilts may be due in large part to the endless possibilities in both size and design. Tracing the changes in quilts from pre-Revolutionary America to the present art-quilt movement shows that on the average there are noticeable variations about every ten years. In each decade quilters seem to go back to earlier ideas and redesign anew from them. Very little in quilt design is entirely new, but there is always a freshness caused by new fabric designs, new techniques, new color combinations and a remarkable inventiveness among quilters.

Mention the words *artist* and *designer* to most quilters and they will tell you that their finished products spring only from availability of fabric and time, not from some special talent or training. Pat Long Gardner's charming handkerchief medallion quilts evolved gradually from a combination of similar full-size quilts of the 18th and 19th Centuries and her passion for doll quilts. Twenty years ago Pat was a collector and maker of quilts and a teacher of those eager to follow in her footsteps. She made afghan-size quilts and tiny perfect doll-bed quilts patterned on traditional designs.

Many of the doll quilts were medallions, allowing a nice central area for a more manageable design to which an attractive border could be added with ease. The step from these designs to similar ones incorporating an ever-growing handkerchief collection was a short one. What better use could anyone find for the handkerchiefs that have been irresistible in shops all over the world or handed down from aunts and grandmothers?! It matters little whether they are printed with scenes from Japan or trimmed in dainty lace and embroidery or made amusing with cartoon designs for children. There is certainly fabric available to use in a charmingly pieced or appliqué border to match any well-designed handkerchief.

Two hundred years ago there were handsome printed squares of fabric depicting heroes and heroines and scenes of battle or bucolic life. These were often incorporated into quilts, creating a perfect central motif for a large bed. For over a hundred years such prints appeared especially at times of great world fairs or the anniversary dates of cities or states or as a means of celebrating political events. Now that most people live in a less grand manner, such elaborate quilts, handsome as they are, have little place in our lives. The design idea, however, seems too good to discard and more suited to our time and space in this charming handkerchief version. It is also the perfect answer to the question of what to do with a beautiful handkerchief lying buried in a dresser drawer.

CARTER HOUCK

"Alpine Village" (Fig. 1)
26″ x 26″
My first Swiss handkerchief given
to me by my son and daughter-in-
law is signed Fisba-Stoffels. The
flowers in the triangle-and-squares
border echo the provincial feel of
the piece. (1983)

1

Hooked on Hankies

I made my first handkerchief quilt more than a decade ago, using a gift handkerchief my son and daughter-in-law had found on their honeymoon trip in Switzerland. Creating a quilt of it, "Alpine Village", (Fig. 1) by adding borders that enhanced the naive scene of a Swiss Alpine village was a great challenge!

Several years later my collection of unusual handkerchiefs had grown to include several other Swiss designs plus Japanese and American, and I was seeing more and more possibilities for designing handkerchief quilts. I grew ever more avid in my search for these interesting small textiles, aided and abetted by well-traveled friends as well as my own foraging in areas near and far.

I found that many varieties of printed handkerchiefs are available, old and new. They are still being printed today by the Swiss, Italians, French, English, and Japanese. The American handkerchiefs I collect, including children's, souvenir, designer signature, floral, landscape, conversational, geometric, and many others, were printed in the 20th Century prior to about 1960. As a collector, I find handkerchiefs of the 19th Century interesting, but their fragility, rarity, and costliness have deterred me from using them in quilts.

American handkerchiefs of the 20th Century are easy to find in thrift shops, flea markets, yard sales, antique shops, and friends' or relatives' handkerchief boxes. Some people seem especially willing to share a handkerchief to be used in a quilt design.

In creating quilts with these small textiles I have almost without trying created a collection that represents the breadth and variety of American handkerchief designs from the 20th Century. In no other area of textile collecting can there be found more interesting varieties of complete designs on cloth in a small size that can be used not only for what they were intended but also for creating beautiful small quilts. Beginning quilters can make hangings designed around handkerchiefs by adding a simple border of squares as I did in the quilt, "Leading the Cows", (Fig. 2) and more advanced quilters can take the idea of any given handkerchief and run with it. The quilts selected for this book are meant to show how to use handkerchiefs as a springboard for creating your own designs.

One of the appeals of using handkerchiefs in designing quilts is the many styles and themes from which to choose. If the occasion calls for something sweet and sentimental, there is a handkerchief for it. If you wish to try something with a contemporary, Oriental, art deco, or folk art theme, that also is possible. There are romantic, geometric, floral, and children's handkerchiefs to choose from. In fact, there is every kind of design or subject from the Bayeaux Tapestry to the comic strip Archie, from a map of the state of Georgia to rules for the game of Canasta, from a horoscope to a Valentine. There is even a handkerchief design that is a calorie counter.

The relatively low cost of collecting handkerchiefs is appealing in an era when so many collectibles keep rising in price. By using some of the scraps you already have, and a minimum of new fabric, making a handkerchief quilt is very affordable. An added bonus is the low expenditure of time necessary to complete these small projects.

Perhaps the biggest appeal of all to me is the chance these quilts give me to experiment with types of design in a small format. I have enjoyed trying out such varied ideas as a color wash, asymmetric borders, Oriental themes, dimensional effects, and still other designs that I can complete fairly quickly.

When there is an occasion to be marked, such as a retirement, a special birthday, a housewarming, or a group challenge project, what could be more apt than a handkerchief quilt? In an era when we are all too busy, it is nice to contemplate a project that is so personal, yet can be finished without undue stress— and without taking much space.

Because so many of us do our quilting on the run, these small designs make ideal traveling companions. They don't add much weight to one's luggage nor drain too much of one's funds. Moreover, in a day and age of so much duplication of design it is refreshing to work with one-of-a-kind small textiles.

I hope you will have as much fun designing and making these quilts as I have, as well as the fun of looking for interesting

"Leading the Cows" (Fig. 2)
15½" x 15½"

A Swiss handkerchief design based on the custom of driving cattle to pasture. The poya or paintings representing this pastoral event are represented in the handkerchief. (1988)

(Fig. 3)

19th and early 20th Century handkerchiefs including a mourning handkerchief.

handkerchiefs. Each time I start a new handkerchief quilt and tell my friends that this is absolutely the last one I'm going to do, they react with raised eyebrows and polite snickers.

Obviously it's the wide diversity of designs that I can't resist. There is little possibility of doing a quilt like anyone else's. Handkerchief quilts also fit in very well with my style of quiltmaking, which is to have a half dozen projects, large and small, going at any given time. They can be done quickly and simply or, if you like, lavished with detail. The choice is yours. I think you will enjoy making these small graphic treasures. The only problem I can foresee is that you might get hooked on them.

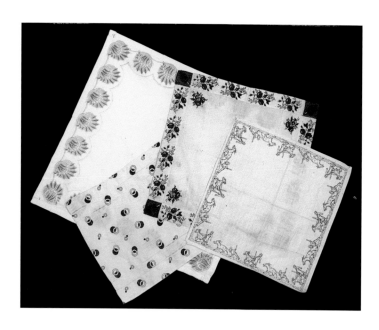

2

A Pocket Size History of the Handkerchief

Long before they made their way into quilts, handkerchiefs served other purposes.

Cloths, which were the predecessors of our present day handkerchiefs, were used as early as the First Century B.C. by the upper classes in Rome. In the Third Century A.D. it was customary to use such cloths to express applause during the gladiator games.

In France, by the 14th Century, handkerchiefs were listed in inventories. Handkerchiefs by this time reflected a growing interest in cleanliness and elegance. In England a handkerchief was called a "hand cloth" or "hand coverchief." By the 16th Century the term "handkerchief" appears in written accounts. The custom of giving handkerchiefs as gifts for weddings, which began in that period, is still practiced in our country today.

By the 18th Century, handkerchiefs were commonly used among all classes of society in the United States and Europe. The use of handkerchiefs when taking snuff coincided in the 18th Century with the revolutionary new process of copperplate printing. These printed handkerchiefs, 27 to 29 inches square, were large enough to cover up snuff-induced sneezes, and the patterned fabric helped camouflage stains.

Printed handkerchief production followed the general history of printed cloth. Copperplate printing and early block printing were followed by roller printing, a more mechanized method of printing that reduced the cost of printing fabrics. Cheaply printed cottons, in turn, made possible a change in the type of printed designs. The 18th-Century copperplate images of George Washington, calendars, and maps gave way in the 19th Century to all kinds of popular motifs. Children's cotton handkerchiefs, for example, were printed with scenes from American sports, games, and children's books. Poetry, music, the alphabet, numbers, and animal themes were also used to convey child-rearing maxims. Such qualities as industry, temperance, and patriotism were considered suitable virtues to be impressed on young minds (Fig. 3).

Handkerchiefs for adults were equally overt in the messages they sent. American heroes, battles, holidays, memorials, political events, and illustrations from popular books were widely depicted on handkerchiefs.

As in other decorative arts, such as china and yard goods, European manufacturers made a point to print handkerchiefs for the American market with subjects related to our history and politics. These motifs continued into the 20th Century and were supplemented in time by newer subjects such as comic strip and movie characters, cowboys, Girl and Boy Scouts, novels, and war themes. The 20th Century also spawned the designer, or signature, handkerchief which was probably related to the signature

(Fig. 4)
Handkerchief designs created by Tammis Keefe—a well known designer in the 1950s.

(Fig. 5)
A group of mid-20th Century handkerchiefs designed by Faith Austin.

"Dancing Elephant"
19" x 19"
By Pat Gardner. (1991)

"Spencer's Quilt" (Fig. 6)
14½" x 14½"
By Liz Jensen. (1991)
These handkerchiefs were designed and signed by Tom Lamb, a children's book illustrator of the 1920s and 1930s. The handkerchiefs of the elephant design are different colorways of the one in the quilt.

(Fig. 7)
Children's handkerchiefs representative of styles from the early 1900s to the 1950s and '60s.

(Fig. 8 and **Fig. 9)**
Two handkerchief gift boxes and a small handkerchief laundry bag fashioned in shirt form with the inscription typed on a paper label affixed to the front: "When your hankies have done their work, Just put them in this little shirt, Stuff them in and let them stay, Till you send your wash away."

scarf. Early designers of scarves for women were Chanel, Patou, Fath, and Worth, French couturiers who were followed by American designers later in the century. One American designer of scarves in the 1950s, Tammis Keefe, was also a prolific designer of handkerchiefs (Fig. 4). Other American handkerchief designers who signed their work were Peg Thomas, Pat Prichard, Rutherford, Billie Kompa, Kati, Monique, and Faith Austin (Fig. 5). Tom Lamb, a children's book illustrator of the 1920s and 1930s, designed whimsical handkerchiefs for children (Fig. 6). Grace Dayton, another children's book illustrator who is known as the originator of the Campbell Soup Kids, designed handkerchiefs in the early 1900s.

A cartoonist, Carl Schultze, who drew the character Foxy Grandpa at the beginning of the 20th Century, signed his handkerchiefs "Bunny" with a drawing of a bunny. Other cartoonists—Chick Young with Blondie, Elzie Segar with Popeye, and later Walt Disney Studios—produced an array of characters that appeared on handkerchiefs in the tradition of the Punch and Judy characters of a century before (Fig. 7).

From the 1930s to the 1950s there was such a myriad of designs—souvenir scenes of cities and states, floral designs, geometrics, and many others—that they spawned accessories such as handkerchief cases, boxes, caddies, laundry bags, handkerchief dolls, and aprons (Fig. 8) (Fig. 9). The once thriving industry came on hard times, alas, with the advent of more convenient, hygienic paper tissue. One can't help wondering if the current concern over environmental issues might not make handkerchiefs viable again.

In the late 18th Century, squares printed specifically for centers of quilts by such well-known American printers as John Hewson of Philadelphia may have inspired later quiltmakers to use handkerchiefs in a central medallion style.

Handkerchiefs were used to make American quilts as early as the beginning of the 19th Century. Later when handkerchiefs were printed in a series of children's book illustrations or a series of political themes, they became incorporated in block design quilts in which a different handkerchief was used in each unit or block. In the quilt revival of the 1930s, floral motif handkerchiefs were also used in block style quilts. Examples of 19th Century quilts made with handkerchiefs may be seen in the collections of the Baltimore Museum of Art, the Museum of American Folk Art, the Shelburne Museum, the Smithsonian Institution, and the Helen Foresman Spencer Museum of Art, as well as in numerous private collections.

The handkerchiefs that I use in my handkerchief quilts span an 80-year period and cover an enormous variety of textile design. In addition to the American handkerchiefs I have used dating from about 1910 to 1960, I have also used handkerchiefs, as I indicated, from England, France, Switzerland, Italy, and Japan that are being printed today. Incorporating these many types of motifs and designs into quilts can make a keen challenge of finding compatible fabric. Even though I have several thousand different patterned fabrics, I often will purchase a few new pieces for each quilt I make. The leftover pieces then become part of my printed fabric repertoire. I usually buy ½-yard pieces unless I am buying fabric for a border or back. I store my fabrics, graded by color, on the shelves of a glass-fronted bookcase where they are easily visible.

The choice of compatible fabric is so important to the success of a handkerchief quilt that I am devoting all of the next chapter to it. After fabric, I take up the subject of color, followed by a chapter on design and technique and lastly the often neglected subject of the actual quilting and the making of its designs. The last chapter supplies diagrams for actual patterns for borders and block designs, corner medallions, and asymmetric designs.

3

Fabric:
Fountain of Ideas

Like many quiltmakers, my primary source of inspiration is the fabric I use. Whether it is a piece of cloth I already own that is perfect for a quilt at hand, or whether it is a new piece that speaks to me from the shelf of a shop or a flea market, the acquiring of fabrics is a constant and rewarding part of the creative process. The fabric can be a gift that evokes memories of the giver. It can be a scrap picked up from the floor of a factory or even the belt that a kind friend takes off the dress she is wearing (as my friend Drusilla once did). In creating textile designs, particularly of patchwork, all of such sources are as much a part of the mystique of the quilt as the design itself.

I particularly like printed fabrics because they evoke so many kinds of style images, running the gamut from conservative mini dots to the wildest Hawaiian fantasies. Printed paisley, geometric, provincial, and art deco designs, as well as conversational or theme prints, ethnic, period, and floral designs of all scales and sizes, both naturalistic and abstract—the choice seems boundless. There are directional prints and all-over designs printed on linen, cotton, wool, and rayon cloth, applied with various techniques such as screen or resist printing, or roller printing on garment or furnishing fabrics.

Cotton cloth currently printed in the United States, Japan, England, France, Switzerland, and Italy is available to quilters both here and on their travels. For those who don't care to shop or who live in isolated areas, there are many fine mail-order companies offering a wide variety. In addition you can find feed sacks and other Depression-era fabrics along with rarer turn-of-the-century fabrics at flea markets, estate sales, and antique shows.

As wide as these choices appear to be, they of course are not all available simultaneously. It therefore behooves the serious quiltmaker to build up her collection of printed fabric, overlooking no opportunity to add to her collection or to begin one. Do we need any more excuse than that?

Recently a friend of mine was given six large cartons of fabric by her church to sell to raise money. She invited me to check them out for quilt possibilities. With the help of a quilting colleague I selected about a hundred two- to three-yard remnants. Many of the printed designs were wild and exotic florals. Some were nautical and juvenile prints, and a few were smaller scale florals and stripes. We had no trouble selling these prints to a group of quilters who are open to the possibilities in non-traditional printed fabrics.

Perhaps we need to remind ourselves that many of our most revered antique quilts were made of non-traditional fabrics. Quilts of the early 19th Century utilized large scale chintzes, plaids, rainbow prints, eccentric prints, and other types of printed designs. Many quiltmakers from this period appeared to have had open minds about prints and patterns. After the advent in the second half of the 19th Century of readily available, inexpensive calicos and small scale floral prints, these became the fabric of choice of many quilters. Notable exceptions to the calicos and floral prints are the varied fabrics found in late 19th- and early 20th-Century scrap quilts and the furnishing fabrics on the backs and occasionally the fronts of some quilts from that period.

The crazy quilts of the late 19th Century used non-traditional fabrics of silks and satins and were the art quilts of their time. Charm quilts of about the same time are notable for the wide variety of printed cottons used in innovative ways. Such fabrics as feed sack material, art deco prints, and a distinctive pastel color palette help to identify quilts made during the Depression.

I think that many of us are grateful for the increasingly varied fabric designs that are now available in quilt shops around the country. As a veteran customer who remembers the onset of these specialty shops in the 1970s, I can see a remarkable improvement in the kind and variety of the selections offered. As good as many of these shops are, and as service oriented as they are and worthy of support, we need to look at still other possibilities for acquiring fabric. Don't overlook the chance of finding fabric at any kind of store from chain household goods stores to the one-room family owned businesses that still exist in isolated areas here and abroad catering to local trade. Once I stumbled upon a dry-goods store that was operated by two Amish sisters in a room in their home.

Along with the fabric, thread, and other findings was a wonderful assortment of handmade booties, children's coloring books, home-made noodles, and men's handkerchiefs. I found several fabrics there which evoke pleasant memories of the occasion.

A well-traveled friend of mine once came upon a cache of fabric in a dingy general store on the island of Hawaii. I will never forget a small family-run department store in a small town in Ireland that yielded beautiful fabrics and impeccable service and extended its hours to accommodate the American tourists in our group. I have also found fascinating fabric in open-air markets in Switzerland, England, and the United States.

About eight years ago a group of us from Baltimore went to Richland, Pennsylvania, to my mother's church to attend a sale of hundreds of bolts of shirting fabrics, contributed to the church by a local shirt manufacturer who had gone out of business. We were able to identify the stripes and plaids of those fabrics in our quilts for years afterwards.

Don't overlook the possibility of finding fabric at your local thrift shops or yard sales, and while you are searching for fabrics, keep your eyes open for interesting handkerchiefs as well. I once lived in a community in which a neighborhood yard sale was an annual event. Those of us in the know went first to the man in the neighborhood who was a fabric sales representative and could be counted on to have samples for sale.

Some of the most wonderful fabrics in my collection were gifts from friends' scrap bags. Probably the ultimate cache of all was a lard stand I was given which contained an assortment of

"Shall We Dance?" (Fig. 10)
20″ x 20″
An Art Deco design depicting
dramatic shapes of dancers. The
border design is an asymmetric
setting of graduated size borders.
(1992)

late 19th- and early 20th-Century sewing scraps. An acquaintance from Denmark generously contributed a large assortment of Danish and American sewing scraps, and my sister who is an interior designer gives me samples from time to time. One of my students made a gorgeous quilt, the envy of us all, using a decorator's sample book of fine French fabrics.

Putting It Together

To give you an example of choosing specific fabrics for a specific quilt, I have chosen the piece I call "Shall We Dance?" (Fig. 10). It has an art deco appearance, so I chose a fan-shaped print by J. Gutcheon Fabrics for the outermost border and a decorator fabric for the inside border.

In an exercise in the possibilities of fabric choice I took this same art deco handkerchief and created another frame for it, using the same color placement and border design but showing two very different fabric design choices (Fig. 11). In the second arrangement of fabrics (Fig. 12), which I think is equally successful, I used a large scale black-and-white print on the border of flowers and leaves and a red South Seas print to create a more contemporary look. An oversized black and white polka-dotted fabric seemed a good choice for the back of this version.

The fabrics in the Japanese quilt, "Haiku", (Fig. 13) are an assortment of English Liberty fabrics, American RJR fabrics, Japanese yukato cloth, and others. The wide assortment of styles, all with an Oriental flavor, works in this crazed patchwork border.

The outside border of "Dogwood Blossoms" (Fig. 14) is an Alexander Henry fabric that picks up the sparkling colors in the handkerchief. In this quilt I selectively cut the border fabric to maximize the vibrancy of the handkerchief.

Sometimes finding the right fabric for a particular quilt is pure serendipity. For example I found a fabric in Charleston, South Carolina, with a design of fish, sea shells, and star fish that complemented a handkerchief designed by Australian designer Ken Done that I used in the quilt called "Barrier Reef" (Fig. 15). For the quilt, "Monkey Business", (Fig. 16) which was designed around a French child's handkerchief, a fabric in my own collection, an Alexander Henry jungle print with monkeys, was a perfect choice for the border.

"Sleeping Beauty" (Fig. 17) was designed around a child's handkerchief from the 1940s. I used a Depression-era fabric of roughly the same period, some men's shirting, and an imported cotton. In the quilt "Foxy Grandpa" (Fig. 18) I used a handkerchief by designer cartoonist Bunny. Selections of fabric from my lard stand collection of late 19th- and early 20th-Century fabrics and some American reproduction fabrics worked well in this quilt.

The quilt, "French Provincial", (Fig. 19) was created using my ten-year collection of French fabric sample swatches. The Pierre Deux border strips complete this French country design.

In the quilt, "Hand and Hearts", (Fig. 20) the sentimental theme of the handkerchief with its symbols of an engagement

(Fig. 11)

Frame of quilt using one assortment of fabrics.

(Fig. 12)

Frame of quilt with other choices.

"Haiku" (Fig. 13)
24" x 24"

The name of this piece refers to the haiku poems written in Japanese characters on the surface of the handkerchief. This handkerchief, a gift, is a well known design of a high class woman dressed elaborately. The fractured border done in the press pieced technique was inspired by Oriental crazy patchwork. (1991)

ring, bluebirds, and cupids relates thematically to the bluebirds and flowers in the printed borders.

In building a fabric collection of many different designs, tone on tone, plaids and stripes, geometrics, large and small scale prints, theme prints, etc., I try to keep in mind that this is a long-range investment, just as making a quilt is a long-range project. Over the years, styles of designs change, and we are all influenced by what is currently fashionable. However, it would be a mistake to clear out the fabrics that don't seem as appealing currently because they may be just the fabrics needed to enhance a future project.

The memories that are evoked by the various fabrics in your collection, no less than the fabrics themselves, are an important part of any composition that you do. If I am making a quilt for a specific person, I try to incorporate some fabrics that are pertinent to that person's history. In "A Wedding Trophy", (Fig. 21) a quilt for my daughter Amanda and her husband Rick, I used a piece of shirting of mine, and one of her father's, as well as the wedding handkerchief given to her by her grandmother to create a personal memento of her wedding.

In addition to using appropriate fabric designs in any single quilt, I think they should as much as possible reflect a variety of motifs: stripes, geometrics, floral, large and small scale, plaids, and so on. Don't overlook the possibilities of selectively cutting out sections of a large scale print. If you choose to make your border of a single-printed fabric, you can use it to make a statement about the total character of a piece. The full-blown roses in the outside border of "Tulips and Roses" (Fig. 22), echoing the showy tulips in the handkerchief, express flowers. The multifloral inner and outer border of "Springtime in New York" (Fig. 23) speak for the season.

In choosing fabrics save some thought for the back of the quilt. Although it is always safe to carry over some of the same fabrics from the front of the quilt, it can be different to use something a little wild on the back. Some people go so far as to create a separate design for the back. The simple pieced design I used for the back of "Study in Blues" (Fig. 24) carries to the back the design theme of the front. On two quilts, "Koala Bears" (Fig. 25) and "Shall We Dance?", I placed another related handkerchief on the back. By pure chance I found a print of Victorian furniture to use on the back of my quilt, "Furniture Gallery" (Fig. 26).

To make your quilt truly distinctive beware of being caught up in the latest popular trend in printed fabrics, whether it be marbleized fabrics, plaids, or large scale prints. By all means include those fabrics in your repertoire, but consider them only a part of the overall picture. Remember also that your quilt should reflect your own style of quiltmaking. Finally, enjoy the adventure of putting your fabrics together. Just as you had fun selecting the fabrics, now enjoy putting them together in a design. Take a chance: Create something that only you can make.

"Dogwood Blossoms" (Fig. 14)
24" x 24"

This is a typical American handkerchief with an Oriental air,
mid-20th Century. (1991)

"Barrier Reef" (Fig. 15)
22" x 22"

Designed by Ken Done, this
handkerchief vividly depicts the
forms of fish and aquatic life on a
barrier reef. The piece is completed by the use of fabric with
sea life and strip pieced rectangles.
(1990)

"Monkey Business" (Fig. 16)

25½" x 25½"

This child's handkerchief, brought
to me by a friend from Mulhouse,
France, is set in a traditional quilt
block and bordered by a jungle
print with monkeys. (1990)

"Sleeping Beauty" (Fig. 17)
18″ x 18″

A children's handkerchief given to me by Betty Kilker. It was hers in the 1940s. (1990)

"Foxy Grandpa" (Fig. 18)
22″ x 22″

Signed by cartoonist Carl Schultze, who used the logo "Bunny" with the symbol of a rabbit to sign his work, this handkerchief was printed in the early 20th Century. The fabrics in the border include a few from that period. (1990)

"French Provincial" (Fig. 19)
33″ x 33″

This handkerchief-scarf, manufactured by Souleiado, is based on old designs from Provence in the south of France. The border design of diagonal rectangles is made of French fabric samples. (1991)

"Hand and Hearts" (Fig. 20)
19″ x 19″

This handkerchief design from the second quarter of the 20th Century incorporates symbols of an engagement, cupids, ring, love-birds. The hearts in the border reflect the theme of the handkerchief. (1991)

"A Wedding Trophy" (Fig. 21)
19″ x 19″

Made for Amanda and Rick Shultz as a wedding memento and signed with their names and the year of their marriage. The handkerchief, a gift to Amanda Long by her grandmother, Margaret Zug, was worn at her wedding. It is surrounded by a ribbon border. (1988)

"Tulips and Roses" (Fig. 22)
31½″ x 31½″

This was designed as a companion
piece to a large quilt—a nine-
patch exchange. The handkerchief
is American, third quarter 20th
Century. Nine patches set on
point form the border. (1992)

"Springtime in New York" (Fig. 23)
24″ x 24″

A quilt show in New York, 1991, yielded this handkerchief with its springtime colors. The pieced borders are fence-shaped. (1991)

"Study in Blues" (Fig. 24)

21″ x 22½″

The asymmetric design of this handkerchief, combined with Japanese yukato and American fabrics, is augmented by further asymmetric placement of geometric shapes in a contemporary arrangement. (1991)

"Furniture Gallery" (Fig. 26)
25" x 25"

Another handkerchief by the designer Tammis Keefe (1950s) reflects the colors and the vernacular of that era. The border design echoes the architectural elements in the handkerchief. The back is a print of furniture. (1991)

"Koala Bears" (Fig. 25)
20" x 20"

Ken Done, an Australian, designed this handkerchief which was a gift from a friend. The border of appliqued leaves echoes the simple shapes of the leaves in the handkerchief. (1991)

"Color Wash" (Fig. 27)

24½″ x 24½″

This gift of a Japanese handkerchief is one that was sold through the Museum of Fine Arts, Boston, and carries their logo. I used many English prints to create the color wash effect in light and dark. (1991)

4

Color: The Instinctive Approach

My own use of color is instinctive, not theoretical. I try first of all to start with the colors that are in the handkerchief and pull out as many possibilities as possible. The more fabrics that are used in a piece, the more latitude there is for blending colors. This is especially true in planning light, medium, and dark values of a color. A few medium tones placed with the light section or the dark section help to move your eye around the piece. When you use many fabrics, colors do not have to match so exactly. That's why the piece, "Color Wash", (Fig. 27) was so satisfying to work on. A quilt such as "Shall We Dance?" is much more limited in its possibilities. In that kind of piece, the light and dark values and contrast are very important.

Sometimes the use of color is so greatly affected by one's own color likes and dislikes that one is forced to confront one's own prejudices. For example in the quilt, "Cloisonne", (Fig. 28) I was forced to use a background fabric for the areas behind the fans that included a large amount of purple (a fabric chosen by my class for a challenge project). By playing up the reds, blues, and turquoise in the Japanese handkerchief, I was able to play down the purple, which I dislike, and achieve a richer effect and one that pleased me.

One of the effects of color on a quilt that I find most interesting is the way the colors draw your eye from one area to another. Yellow is a color that is compelling in a design and should be used sparingly. The gold and yellow stars in the pieced star border of "Stars Around the Nativity" (Fig. 29) that twinkle around the border reflect the golden stars in the handkerchief. A few yellow squares in "Swiss Costumes" (Fig. 30) give it sparkle as well.

In creating my handkerchief quilts I find myself much more open to color as it fits a particular handkerchief design. Perhaps because of the small size of the pieces, I do not feel that every handkerchief quilt I make has to relate to a room in my house or a design scheme. I am free to select a handkerchief simply because I like it and can create a design that pleases me.

Some people find that it is a help to think of light, medium, and dark values when planning a particular design. In the quilt "Fireworks" (Fig. 31) the dark valued triangles are shooting out from the center, the lighter valued triangles are pointing to the center. Medium values of color can be used on either the dark side or the light side of the design, intermittently, to achieve a more subtle effect than a stark contrast of light and dark throughout. In manipulating color tones of light, medium, and dark, the more solid tone on tone prints are easier to work with.

My own approach to color placement in a quilt is to place the color pieces individually in the borders I use. This gives me

"Cloisonne" (Fig. 28)

26″ x 26″

Another Japanese handkerchief given to me by a friend was used in a mystery challenge quilt in 1989. The design is set on point with double fans on the corners. (1989)

"Stars Around the Nativity"
(Fig. 29)
21" x 21"
The design of this handkerchief
has a south-of-the-border appearance, although it was found in a
flea market in Maryland. The design of stars for the border reflects
the spirit of the occasion. (1991)

a freedom to arrange and rearrange them until they please me. If I am using pieced blocks, I arrange the pieced blocks rather than the individual squares or triangles, but I always arrange the whole quilt on the wall on my flannel sheet. In this way I can maneuver the pieces until I make my final arrangement and sew them to-gether.

The placement of color in my quilts is one of the most satisfying parts of the process for me. I am in no rush to hasten this part but take my time to savor the pleasure of manipulating the colors. After all, I am creating this piece for my own enjoy-ment and to suit my own aesthetic sensibilities.

Because I love working with color, I enjoy picking up the colors in the handkerchiefs I use in creating these small quilts. There are as many color schemes possible as there are handker-chiefs. I currently have five or six bags of handkerchiefs with compatible fabric choices ready to select the one that appeals to me most to work on next.

In choosing colors to use in a composition, I try to keep an open mind about trying many possibilities. I have learned through my teaching that there are many ways to achieve an interesting effect. I would like to warn you about taking too literally the matching of a flower in one fabric with a stripe in another. The overall effect is what counts. One tool that I find helpful in achieving this overall effect is a reducing glass, available in any art store, which helps you to see the way the colors blend as if from a distance. Better still, if you have the space, stand back from your quilt and squint.

In making color choices for a handkerchief quilt, I lay the handkerchief on a table and pull out from my collection of fabrics a variety of types of prints and light and dark colors that pick up those in the handkerchief (Fig. 32). I begin with eight or ten fabrics that are compatible. Then I go back to my stack of fabrics and look again for other possible choices. After I've done this several times, I know whether I have enough of a selection to create a design that uses many shades and different fabrics or one that only requires a few. In the quilt "Shall We Dance?" I had a limited selection of black and clear red fabrics on hand, so I settled for only nine different fabrics in that piece. The simple asymmetric border design maximized the effect of these few fabrics.

With the blue and red Japanese handkerchief in the quilt, "Color Wash", I used over a hundred different printed fabrics from my large collection of blue and red printed fabrics. To achieve more variation, I placed the square template in several areas of a large scale multi-colored fabric. This gave me several different squares out of one fabric. I created the effect of a color wash by shading the blue, red, and gold fabrics from dark values to light in opposite corners. A plus in this design occurred spontaneously where the flowers in the handkerchief appear to bleed into the border.

Because there were so many colors in the handkerchief I used to create "Stars Around the Nativity", I had many options in my fabric choices. "Koala Bears" and "Swiss Costumes" are other examples of handkerchiefs that have a wide range of colors in their design. In all of these I placed the colors around the border

"Swiss Costumes" (Fig. 30)

21½″ x 21½″

The costumes shown on this
handkerchief are similar to costumes found in the Swiss Costume
Museum in Lucerne. The squares
in the border incorporate some
Swiss fabrics. (1987)

"Fireworks" (Fig. 31)

19½" x 19½"

The center of this handkerchief
explodes toward a border of flowers. The border design picks up
the explosion on another level.
(1990)

"Shall We Dance?" (Fig. 32)
A selection of fabrics and the handkerchief.

"The Three Sisters" (Fig. 33)
25″ x 25″
This Japanese handkerchief was given to me by a friend who found it in Hawaii. The border is a ribbon design. (1989)

"Marching Bear" **(Fig. 34)**

18½″ x 18½″

Another design by Tom Lamb—a
children's handkerchief from the
1930s. (1990)

"Bows from Sedona" (Fig. 35)
24" x 24"
The bows printed on this handkerchief found in Sedona, Ari-
zona, were scaled up to form the
four corners of the design. (1991)

"Japanese Medallion" (Fig. 36)

25½" x 25½"

This Japanese handkerchief, a gift
from a friend, has a formal sym-
metrical design with gold paint
highlighting some of the motifs.
The border is diagonal strip piecing. The family name for this
quilt is "Bill's Triple Bypass".
(1990)

"Hearts and Flowers" (Fig. 37)
24½″ x 24½″
By Thelma Scott. It was made by
Thelma for a friend whose son
brought her the handkerchief from
England. (1991)

"Apples and Arrows" (Fig. 38)
22½" x 22½"

This is a handkerchief designed by
Peg Thomas, mid-20th Century,
in which the motifs of apples and
arrows are repeated in the pieced
arrow border and quilted apples in
the corners. (1990)

in a random mix of light and dark in different hues on all four sides.

In other handkerchief quilts such as "The Three Sisters", (Fig. 33) "The Marching Bear", (Fig. 34) and "Fireworks" I placed the fabrics in the border in consecutive order on each side of the quilt in a repeated arrangement of lights and darks.

Quilts such as "Study in Blues" and "Bows from Sedona" (Fig. 35) are essentially monochromatic and rely on the scale and variety of printed designs of the fabric as well as light and dark contrast to achieve an interesting effect.

The beautiful handkerchief that I used in "Japanese Medallion" (Fig. 36) was one of the most difficult to work with. The colors and design of the handkerchief were so classic and beautiful that I felt inhibited until I started experimenting with a simple diagonal strip-pieced border in which I used a brighter version of the colors in the quilt. This experiment created more depth and kept the quilt from being too predictable. Thelma Scott in her quilt, "Hearts and Flowers", (Fig. 37) achieved a similar effect of depth by floating a light colored plain border between two dark pieced borders.

One strategy that I find useful in determining color placement is to place the pieces of fabric on the previously mentioned flannel sheet that hangs on the wall in my studio. I may leave a piece that I am undecided about with two or three possibilities in place on the wall while I live with it for a few days or until I decide that I am satisfied with the result. Sometimes comments from quilting friends or from family members can be helpful at this point to help me clarify my own ideas. I don't worry about cutting too many squares or blocks. They can be used in future projects.

Just as certain designs in fabric go in and out of style, so do colors. Buy a favorite while it is currently available. That special shade of turquoise that you love may not be available next year.

Although I find myself drawn to certain colors and combinations of color, I try to be open to new possibilities. The times I struggle with not having enough of a certain fabric to finish my plan often result in a quilt that is more vital than one that is too carefully coordinated. A careful study of antique scrap quilts provides insight into how a minus can turn into a plus. Some of the improvisations that early quiltmakers were forced to make resulted in quilts that are exciting and beautiful. There are no hard and fast rules. Don't be afraid to let yourself go.

5

Design and Techniques

My ideas and suggestions on design, as on color, are intended to be used as a springboard for creating your own designs. Because the handkerchiefs I have used vary in size from 8 to 28 inches square, it is impossible to draw a specific size pattern for all quilts. Then, too, the designs of handkerchiefs vary and need to be related to the border designs. Therefore, I can only convey some general instructions that would apply to all handkerchief quilts.

The handkerchiefs themselves are usually printed on a light-weight, finely woven linen or cotton. If you are working with an old handkerchief, check it for condition, making sure there are no small stains or holes. If there is a hand-rolled hem, rip it out carefully, wash the handkerchief, and press it. You should now have an adequate seam allowance available to construct your first inside border.

Select a narrow, ¼-inch to 1¼-inch wide inside border. This first border provides a stable, firmer material on which to sew your subsequent borders, as well as an aesthetic definition of the handkerchief itself. You can use this first border to manipulate

"Let's Play Ball" **(Fig. 39)**
24½" x 24½"

This handkerchief was created by
Tammis Keefe, a prolific designer
in San Francisco in the 1950s.
The pieced border represents a
fence around the ball field. (1991)

"The Aviary of Bird Fancyers Recreation" (Fig. 40)
38″ x 38″

This gentleman's snuff handkerchief is a replica of an 18th Century copperplate printed textile in the Williamsburg collection. The original, bearing the engraver's signature, was printed in England.

There is a fascinating array of captions of 13 different kinds of birds and an illustration of capturing birds for use as pets. The pieced border design is "Wild Goose Chase". (1991)

the size of the center square to make an even number of inches that will make it easier to draft the subsequent borders. For instance, an 8½-inch square handkerchief could be made into a 9-inch center square by using a ¼-inch first border, or the same 8½-inch handkerchief could be made into a 10-inch center square by using a ¾-inch inside border. Any even number of inches is easier to work with in drafting subsequent borders. The size of the first or inside border should be an aesthetic as well as a practical decision.

Now you are ready to decide whether the handkerchief design would work better as a medallion with borders or a medallion with corner designs or a traditional block design. If you feel adventurous you might consider creating your own one-of-a-kind off-center, asymmetric design.

There are many different border designs commonly used in making quilts, but before you decide to go with one of the old standbys, consider the design of the handkerchief. Are there any motifs that could be lifted out of the handkerchief itself, such as the one I evolved in my quilt "Apples and Arrows" (Fig. 38)? My border design used pieced arrows with apples quilted on the corners. The pieced arrows were readily charted on graph paper.

The appliqued leaves in the border of "Koala Bears" repeated the shape of the leaves in the handkerchief. In "Let's Play Ball" (Fig. 39) I designed a border that created an illusion of a fence around the ball park.

For some borders the border design is more a matter of semantics than an actual replica of a motif. In "The Aviary" (Fig.

40) the border I chose was the traditional design Wild Goose Chase. In "Stars Around the Nativity" I used the block design called Milky Way as the border.

Sometimes a traditional border design is the most apt. In the quilt, "French Provincial", the shapes of the diagonally placed rectangles perfectly fitted my collection of French fabric swatches. In Florence Squires's "Imari" (Fig. 41) the fan shapes of the border squares are apropos both of the Oriental theme of the quilt and the scale of the Japanese fabrics used on them.

Two of the handkerchief quilts in this collection use the same border. My quilt, "The Trees", (Fig. 42) with its reverse corner placement blocks looks very different from Barbara McGuinness's "Erin Bagh Sails", (Fig. 43) which has a more nautical look, reminiscent of flags on ships, yet it is the same basic design.

On two other quilts, Monique Thormann's "Tree of Life" (Fig. 44) and Carole Glowacki's "Mateja's Flower Garden", (Fig. 45) the theme of leaves is similar, but each is very different from the other. In Monique's border the leaves are placed randomly at different angles, while Carole uses a more formal arrangement. Each reflects the spirit of the handkerchief it frames.

In yet another parallel of similar design, Betty Ayella's quilt, "Tennis Anyone", (Fig. 46) and my quilt, "Baubles", (Fig. 47) each uses a similar shape unit in the pieced border with narrow plain borders on each side of it. Because of the different handkerchief design and color scheme, the effect is vastly different.

Another interesting border design is Nanette Greif's baroque

"Imari" (Fig. 41)

22" x 22"

By Florence Squire. It was made
using a Japanese handkerchief pur-
chased on a trip to Tokyo in
1991. The pieced border incorporates some Japanese yukato fabrics.
(1991)

"The Trees" (Fig. 42)
22½" x 22½"

The painterly qualities of this
handkerchief from the mid-20th
Century are offset by the geometric border. (1990)

looking curved design that picks up the wheels of the motif in her Japanese handkerchief for her piece "Oriental Fanfare" (Fig. 48). Yvette Howard's piece, "Midnight in Morocco", (Fig. 49) uses a formal arrangement of a design reminiscent of an Oriental rug to enhance her handkerchief.

In Beverly Wohlust's "Circle of Flowers", (Fig 50) repeating the hexagonal shape of the handkerchief in an exquisitely executed, small scale version of Grandmother's Flower Garden is a wonderful choice for this piece.

I particularly like the crazed strip border on the Japanese handkerchief on the quilt that I designed called "Haiku". This border is a traditional design sometimes seen on early Japanese clothing. In Rae Engle's handkerchief quilt, "Plum Blossoms at Nightfall", (Fig. 51) the random strip piecing offers yet another appropriate border for a Japanese design.

If you have decided to go the route of a more elaborate corner medallion design, two options to consider are either to set the handkerchief straight on as in "The Ascent" (Fig. 52) or on point as in "Bows from Sedona". In both of these quilts the corner triangles are pieced. In "The Ascent" the outside triangles are pieced of light and dark triangles that blend with the Swiss handkerchief in the center. In "Bows from Sedona" the handkerchief is set on point, and four pieced large scale bows fill in the corners.

Another option is to use a traditional block design to form the frame for your handkerchief. The star design in "Swiss Chalet" (Fig. 53) is based on the popular Sawtooth Star block. The unit design for "Monkey Business" by the author and "Scottish Banner"

(Fig. 54) by Mary Ann Crawford is based on the same traditional block design.

If you want to start from scratch to create your own design, one suggestion would be to use strips of varying width to create an asymmetric design as I did in "Shall We Dance?" and again in "Dancing Elephant". Or you could try an asymmetric arrangement of stripes, squares, and rectangles as I did in "Study in Blues". There is no end to the possibilities that might occur to you as you get involved in your project. In Sharron Banks's quilt "Broken Promise", (Fig. 55) she divided or cut apart the handkerchief itself to symbolize the theme for the quilt in her avant garde design. She then designed it on her studio wall and sewed it together in the manner of a Log Cabin block, working from the center to the edge.

After you have worked out in your mind what kind of a design to use and you have done the preliminary work of placing the first border around the handkerchief, you are ready to chart the quilt on a piece of graph paper. If you use the scale of one inch to a square, you can readily see whether your border design will fit the number of inches that you need to form the border. Most of the border designs that I have used for these quilts are two or three inches wide, as this scale works well for the size of these pieces. If the number of repeats across does not fit the size of your handkerchief, you can always fill in with plain borders. The designs I have used in this book are readily transferred to graph paper.

The scale of the borders or corners in a medallion style quilt

"Erin Bagh Sails" (Fig. 43)
20″ x 20″
By Barbara McGuinness. This
Swiss handkerchief was given to
Barbara by a friend of hers, Mar-
garet Riehl, who is a fellow quilter
and sailor. It is named for
Barbara's home on the Eastern
Shore of Maryland. (1991)

"Tree of Life" (Fig. 44)

23½" x 23½"

By Monique Thormann. The
handkerchief was given to
Monique by her sister who lives in
Mulhouse, France. (1991)

is one of the most important decisions you will make in designing your quilt. Some of the handkerchiefs that I used are as small as eight or ten inches square, others are as large as 28 inches square. Usually the size of the frame for the piece should be consistent with the size of the handkerchief as well as the printed design on it. For example the diagonally set squares on the border of "Marching Bear" are a size that is apropos of the diagonally set square handkerchief that it is framing. An exception to this is the large scale corner pieced bows in the design "Bows of Sedona" in which the very small printed bows on the handkerchief are considerably enlarged on the corners for a striking effect. The scale of Beverly Wohlust's charming composition, "Circle of Flowers", is appealing in its consistent miniaturization.

A thematic approach to design is especially important in creating these small works. On many of the quilts the theme of the handkerchief is evident in the choice of a border or corner design. In "Fireworks" the elongated triangles reflect the bursting rays in the handkerchief design. The ribbon border on "A Wedding Trophy" as well as Laura Boehl's design, "Roses, Roses, Roses", (Fig. 56) convey an appropriate sentimental message to the viewer. Other themes of flowers and leaves, nautical, Oriental, and animal themes vary with the spirit of the handkerchief itself. It does not have to be as overt a choice as the hearts on the quilt, "Hand and Hearts". It can be more abstract as in the squares surrounding the handkerchief in the piece, "Dogwood Blossoms", in which the fabrics in the squares reflect the flowers in the handkerchief.

In Mary Ann Crawford's quilt, "Scottish Banner", the theme of the stags in the handkerchief, on the fabric on the back, and on the pin with the Crawford crest combine to make this an especially personal quilt. The choice of the design of the setting using simple large triangles showcases the Scottish tartans that reflect the theme of this work.

After you have completed putting your top together and are ready to sandwich the three layers of quilt together, the top, batting, and back, there is one other step I suggest. Check the opacity of your handkerchief by placing it on top of the batting. If it is a white or light background handkerchief and you are placing it on a white batting, there should be no problem. However, if it is a dark colored handkerchief which "washes out" when placed against a light batting, I would suggest using a dark batting or lining the handkerchief.

I really believe that everyone can cultivate a sense of design. I do not have an art background, but I have developed certain strategies that work for me.

One thing I find important is to work quickly when I am inspired by an idea. If it means that a meal is late or my studio or house is a mess, so be it. I am compelled to work quickly to see how my idea develops. I usually work with my design on a wall where I can constantly check its progress and can leave it as long as necessary. Although I may start out with a sketch or a design on graph paper, it is impossible to predict what will happen when I translate the design to printed cloth. I try to be free to make changes as I work. Because making a quilt is such a time

"Mateja's Flower Garden" (Fig. 45)

24" x 24"

By Carole Glowacki. Made by
Carole after the birth of her first
grandchild, Mateja. Her interest
in handkerchief quilts grew out of
a purchase of several handkerchiefs in Switzerland. (1991)

"Tennis Anyone?" (Fig. 46)

22" x 22"

By Betty Ayella. A French handkerchief from the Musee De
L'Impressions Sur Etoffes in Mulhouse inspired this piece. (1991)

"Baubles" **(Fig. 47)**
32″ x 32″
Italian designer Carlos Falchi produced the design for this handkerchief. The shapes in the border
reflect the shapes of the jewels.
(1992)

"Oriental Fanfare" (Fig. 48)
31½″ x 31½″
By Nanette Greif, made from a
Japanese handkerchief designed for
the Boston Museum of Fine Arts.
The border fans are apropos of
Nan's interest in Oriental art.
(1991)

"Midnight in Morocco" (Fig. 49)
34½″ x 32½″
By Yvette Howard. The border
design, which is adapted from a
pattern by Virginia Walton, is
very apt on this handkerchief
made in Switzerland. (1991)

"Circle of Flowers" (Fig. 50)

27″ x 28″

By Beverly Wohlust. The 24 flowers made of ½″ hexagons was inspired by this hexagon shaped handkerchief with its Depression-era colors. (1991)

"Plum Blossoms at Nightfall"
(Fig. 51)
26½" x 26½"
By Rae Engle. The Japanese
handkerchief used in this work
was given to Rae by her daughter
when she lived in Tokyo for several years. (1991)

"The Ascent" (Fig. 52)

34″ x 34″

Signed Fisba-Stoffels, this hand-kerchief depicts the horse and wa-gon loaded with utensils for milk-ing cows and making cheese. It is in the style of the poyas, an art form found in Gruyere. The quilt design is a square-in-square with triangles forming the corners. (1989)

"Swiss Chalet" (Fig. 53)

26½" x 26½"

Signed Lehner, this handkerchief uses many of the symbols used in folk art of the area. The setting of the handkerchief is a sawtooth star. Both the handkerchief and fabrics were acquired on a trip to Switzerland. (1987)

"Scottish Banner" (Fig. 54)

28" x 29"

By Mary Ann Crawford. This
quilt was made as a representation
of a banner that would hang in a
great hall of a castle. The Scottish
tartans and stags enhance the
theme of the quilt, as does the pin
of the Crawford crest placed on
the Crawford tartan. (1991)

consuming activity, it is important in the beginning to spend as much time as you need on the concept of the design.

Once the components or units of the design are in place and I think the design will work, I leave it on the wall yet another day or two in order to do some fine tuning on it. I may rearrange a few blocks or units at this time. I may also invite comments from colleagues, family, or friends. If you decide to get some feedback on your quilt, remember that that is all it is. The ultimate decisions are still yours to make. Perhaps I should mention at this point that I am somewhat of a risk taker. Some of my favorite quilts turn out to have been chances I took or experiments I made.

If I find myself bogged down by an idea that isn't working, I get on to something else. Although I know that many people feel they have to finish every project they start whether they like it or not, I think that is the way to lose a lot of the joy of creating. If you aren't sure that your idea will work, try it on something small. Sometimes putting the whole project aside for a time will generate some new ideas.

Source of Ideas

Where do we get ideas for the quilts that we make? I am inspired by old and new quilts, by paintings, by the colors and forms in nature, by patterns in architecture and on fabric, by geometric units in quilt blocks or tile patterns, by effects of illusion. By educating your eye to be observant of the world around you and keeping a notebook handy to jot down ideas, you will soon have many more than you can use. It will not be necessary then to buy a kit with the decisions already made or to copy someone else's quilt exactly.

After trying a lot of techniques and ideas you will know what you feel comfortable doing. Your quilts will become recognizably yours. Of course this does not mean that your style will not evolve over the years.

I view good technique as something to strive for but not to be obsessed about. I am more interested in the concept of a design than in the way it is executed. But in my own work, I aim to have my technique be smooth enough so that it does not detract from the composition. I think that everyone has his own tolerance level for imperfection. I believe it is better not to compare yourself with other people but to do the best you can and capitalize on your own strengths. If your strength is use of color, play that up. If your strength is drafting and executing perfect geometric shapes, do that. Or if applique appeals to you and you are good at it, develop your own designs for that.

"Broken Promise" (Fig. 55)
35″ x 49″

By Sharron Bank. The artist designed this quilt on the wall using
a clockwise Log Cabin technique.
The narrative quality of this piece
is further enhanced by the fabrics
she chose. (1991)

"Roses, Roses, Roses" (Fig. 56)
29″ x 29″
By Laura Boehl. The rose design
fabrics in the quilt augment the
roses in the handkerchief. Laura's
biggest challenge was to enhance
the design of the handkerchief,
and not to overwhelm it.

In designing quilts I am not trying to convey a message of concern for an issue, nor am I trying to tell a story, or convey an emotion. I am trying to create something beautiful with fabric, particularly patterned fabric, that I hope I will still consider beautiful ten years from now or that perhaps my grandchildren will like. Although I have found lifesaving therapy in designing and making quilts, I prefer to use the process itself for healing, rather than making an overt gesture to a certain occasion in my life. Some people I know have found comfort in a memorial quilt or a divorce quilt. I may refer to one of my handkerchief quilts as "Bill's bypass quilt," but the quilt has no overt images of surgery. For me having something beautiful to work on at a stressful time is of such benefit that I don't need any direct reminder of the occasion. A handkerchief quilt is a nice size quilt to work on at such times, and it can be carried with you and called on almost anywhere for the lift that quilting offers.

6

Quilting: Importance of Its Design

As important as the choices of fabric, color, and design are to creating a quilt, of equal importance is the design of the quilting lines that hold the three layers together. Many an otherwise fine quilt has been minimized by the design and amount of quilting on it.

Let's talk about the amount of quilting first as that is easier to determine. If you are a person who loves to quilt and likes a lot of quilting, by all means lavish your quilt with lots of fine stitching. In addition to the amount of quilting that you do, consider the overall balance or distribution of the quilting lines. It is probably more effective to distribute the quilting evenly throughout the piece than to have scattered, closely quilted motifs with blank areas in between. If you are an adherent of scattered motifs, consider doing some background quilting between the motifs in either straight or curved lines.

I know how tempting it is for many people to buy the ready-made plastic quilting templates, but the chance of finding one that will exactly fit the size and design requirements of your par-

"Japanese Landscape" (Fig. 58)
36″ x 36″

A Japanese handkerchief with the
Boston Museum of Fine Arts logo
reflects the subtle colors of the
Japanese culture. A simple diagonal rectangular border completes
this quilt. (1992)

"Fashion Plate 1931" (Fig. 57)
24″ x 24″

Fisba-Stoffels is the signature on this Swiss handkerchief depicting the fashions of the Thirties. The border is a pieced ribbon design. (1991)

"Merry Christmas" (Fig. 59)
18½″ x 18½″

Tammis Keefe designed this handkerchief in the 1950s. The border design uses Santa Clauses in a ribbon pieced border. (1988)

ticular quilt is remote. It will probably take you less time to draw your own. By looking at the themes in the handkerchief and quilt top and relating the quilting lines to that theme you will achieve a well-blended whole and have the satisfaction of creating a custom fit.

In experimenting with various quilting design possibilities I use a sheet of tracing paper laid over the graphed chart of the quilt top design. I can make as many sketches and lines as occur to me on the sheets of paper without erasing on the fabric until I find the one I think is best. I usually keep my quilting designs pretty simple. There are many patterns that can be made from circles and half circles alone, such as chains, parallel curves, clam shells, fleur-de-lis, and the egg-and-dart motif. A combination of straight lines and curved lines in the quilting adds balance and flow to the overall quilt design.

In some quilts, design motifs for quilting easily suggest themselves, such as the design of arches that I used on the border of the quilt "Fashion Plate 1931", (Fig. 57) which relates to the shapes of the railing behind the figures in that handkerchief. In the quilt "Japanese Landscape", (Fig. 58) I repeated some oval shapes found in the handkerchief in the overlapping ovals on the rectangles of the border. In the same piece the background areas on the handkerchief were divided into three color zones that I quilted in three separate background designs of meandering lines, double diagonal lines, and clam shells.

The handkerchief designer Tammis Keefe's handkerchiefs,

which I made into the quilts called "Furniture Gallery" and "Let's Play Ball" and "Merry Christmas", (Fig. 59) all have centers that I thought lent themselves to the formation of a grid: in the case of "Furniture Gallery", an irregular grid, and in the examples of "Let's Play Ball" and "Merry Christmas", an even or regular grid. In both cases the grid serves to lift up the figures within the grid. In the piece "Furniture Gallery", I again used a grid of diagonal lines to highlight the print in the border fabric which was printed in a regular repeat of motifs. Many printed fabrics lend themselves to this treatment.

One of the basic principles to remember in designing quilting lines is that areas that need to advance or puff out should be quilted around, and areas that need to recede or flatten should be quilted. By quilting around the figures in "The Three Sisters" the shapes of the figures advanced, and by flattening the background area behind the figures with diagonal lines of close quilting I strengthened this effect. In Anne Wiest's quilt "Remembrance", (Fig. 60) she quilted around the flowers in the handkerchief, then created a textured effect on the solid white border, with a closely quilted grid.

Sometimes a more complex effect can be created in the pieced areas by judicious use of extra lines of quilting such as those in the border of my quilt "The Trees". I superimposed squares on the diagonal over the crossed triangular pieced blocks to lend more complexity.

In another attempt at creating an illusion with quilting lines

I alternated the direction of the lines in the fence-like border in the quilt called "Let's Play Ball". These lines lend an appearance of movement or depth.

Occasionally I like to carry the quilting motif from one area of the quilt top design to another. In "Tulips and Hearts" I continued the swag design from the edge of the handkerchief into the first border. This same principle works well in border designs in which there are several plain rows that can be treated as one continuous unit of chain, tile pattern, or even feathered motifs.

Echo quilting, while most commonly associated with Hawaiian quilts, works well with any kind of curved design. I enjoyed using this technique on the center of my quilt "Swiss Costumes". I liked the contrast of the curved center of this quilt with the geometric lines of the border. Echo quilting is pleasant to do because it is easy to eyeball around the motifs in $\frac{1}{4}$-inch or $\frac{1}{2}$-inch spacing. It gives a similar effect to what many quilters get when they outline shapes of squares, triangles, and other components of quilt blocks $\frac{1}{4}$ inch in from the seam.

Occasionally I try my hand at some freehand motifs if the piece suggests it. In a quilt, "The Three Graces", I added a few leaf shapes and fern shapes to fill in some blank areas in the handkerchief. You don't have to have fantastic drawing skills to sketch in a leaf, a flower, or some other simple shape. Try it on paper first so you can check the size and scale of the motif.

An easy way to create a curved design for a square or particular area that you want to fill in with quilting is to cut a piece of paper $\frac{1}{4}$ inch smaller all around than the section to be filled.

Then, keeping in mind the theme of the piece, you can fold the paper several times and with a scissors create a design in the fashion of the snowflakes children used to make. This old technique was used on some of the mid-19th-Century Baltimore Album quilts, and it's easy to do.

Just as it is good to continue a pieced border design around corners, it is also good to continue the quilting design around the corners. To achieve this it is important to measure the size of the repeats so that they will come out even. If your border is 18 inches on each side, a repeat of 2 inches or 3 inches would work. In the example of "Baubles" the parallel half circles that I used began in the center of each outside border section facing the corners to form a circle where it met the half circle from the adjacent side.

I usually mark the quilting lines on the piece before I baste it together if I am sure of the design. If I am not sure, I will work on the area that I am sure about and think about the remaining areas while I quilt the piece. Sometimes I will quilt a small section before I make a decision to use the design. I mark with lead or chalk pencils that erase easily because I don't wash my quilts after I quilt them.

When I quilt a small quilt, I am especially careful to baste the three layers together well to prevent slipping and stretching. On projects made to hang on a wall, I do my best to keep the edges straight, even if it means extra measuring and basting.

I find it ironic that there have been reams of material written about quilting techniques but hardly anything written about creating interesting quilt designs. There is even a mythology about how many stitches per inch is desirable. While the technique of making tiny, even stitches has merit, it doesn't tell the whole story. About 15 years ago when I was viewing a collection of family quilts owned by a Hawaiian woman, I had the temerity to ask her if Hawaiian women used the same goal of 12 stitches per inch that mainland American women were encouraged to aim for. I will never forget the disdainful look she gave me as she said "Hawaiian quilters don't count stitches." I try to keep that in mind when I start getting too worried about my quilting stitches or technique in general. Although I try to do my best in any of the processes of constructing a quilt, I also value the qualities of handmade work that reveal its human origins. Enjoyment of the process is high on my list of priorities as well, and ripping is not enjoyable.

Because of its repetitive nature, quilting can be a very relaxing part of making the quilt. One of quilting's best features is that it can be done in the company of others. As an icebreaker in a public place, be it a waiting lounge or a park bench, it is unparalleled. I have been approached by all kinds of people in different countries as I am quilting. They are invariably friendly, and if they are not quilters themselves, they regale me with stories of their aunts or grandmothers who are. Quilting can help to alleviate some of the stress of waiting for a medical appointment or procedure, a late plane, or the end of a meeting.

Best of all aspects of quilting is the camaraderie that is achieved by a group of quilters who regularly quilt together either on group or individual projects. Historically, women quilting together have raised each other's consciousness about issues such as women's suffrage, the Civil War, and temperance. The members of the quilting group that I have met with on a weekly basis for almost 20 years, "Sept and Quilt", have succored each other through all of life's experiences from birth of children and grand-children, to divorce and separation, to death of family members. In my classes when we share our opinions over questions of design and technique, there is a most refreshing spirit of cooperation and caring for one another and a lack of divisive competition. What other art form or craft embodies a spirit of sharing and cooperation such as that experienced by quilters?

"Remembrance" (Fig. 60)
24″ x 24″
By Anne Wiest. This quilt was
inspired by a handkerchief Anne
inherited from her mother. (1991)

7

Diagrams to Help You Make Your Own Patterns

The first category of diagrams, Border Designs, has been divided into one-, two-, three-, and four-unit segments. This arrangement of numbered units refers to the division of the design into vertical segments. The horizontal arrangement of the space could be more or less than the vertical divisions. The dotted lines indicate how the designs would appear on graph paper and are a guide to drafting your own patterns. In this section I have also included suggestions for corner units or blocks to join the border designs. It is particularly important to correlate the design of the borders in the corners in the event that the border designs are a different horizontal size and would not naturally form their own corner blocks. The drawings refer you by figure numbers to photographs showing uses of the designs in finished quilts.

In the second category of diagrams, Quilt Blocks, I have incorporated the handkerchief in the center square of a traditional block. Many traditional blocks can be used this way.

Medallion Sets, the third category of diagrams, is one in which the handkerchief is centered within corner designs. The handkerchief could be placed either straight on or diagonally. Again, any number of corner designs are possible.

In the fourth category of diagrams, Asymmetric Designs, I have shown random width and graduated size strips of fabrics.

My purpose in providing diagrams instead of ready-made templates is to allow for adjusting the size of the units to the scale of the individual handkerchief in the design you are creating. I hope that you will use these designs more for inspiration and ideas than for making exact replicas. The excitement comes with experimenting!

Border Designs

One-Unit Design

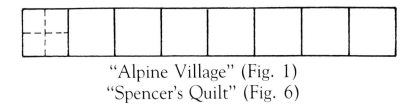

"Alpine Village" (Fig. 1)
"Spencer's Quilt" (Fig. 6)

Two-Unit Designs

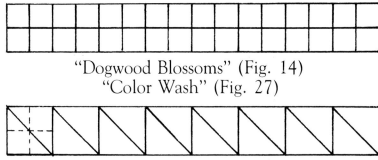

"Dogwood Blossoms" (Fig. 14)
"Color Wash" (Fig. 27)

"Alpine Village" (Fig. 1)

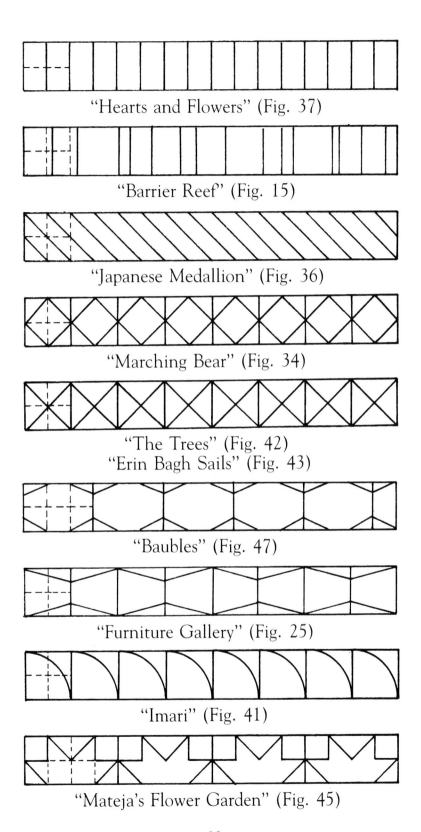

"Hearts and Flowers" (Fig. 37)

"Barrier Reef" (Fig. 15)

"Japanese Medallion" (Fig. 36)

"Marching Bear" (Fig. 34)

"The Trees" (Fig. 42)
"Erin Bagh Sails" (Fig. 43)

"Baubles" (Fig. 47)

"Furniture Gallery" (Fig. 25)

"Imari" (Fig. 41)

"Mateja's Flower Garden" (Fig. 45)

Three-Unit Designs

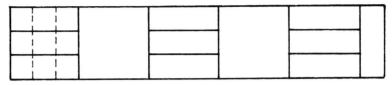

"Merry Christmas" (Fig. 59)

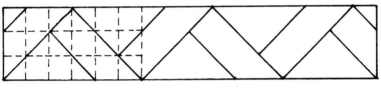

"Apples and Arrows" (Fig. 38)

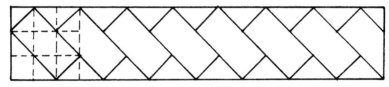

"Fashion Plate 1931" (Fig. 57)
"Roses, Roses, Roses" (Fig 56)
"A Wedding Trophy" (Fig. 21)

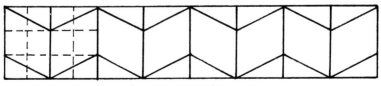

"French Provincial" (Fig. 19)
"Japanese Landscape" (Fig. 58)

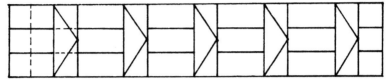

"Let's Play Ball" (Fig. 39)

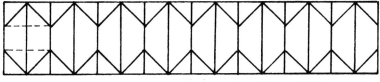

"Springtime in New York" (Fig. 23)

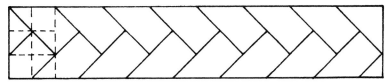

"Foxy Grandpa" (Fig. 18)

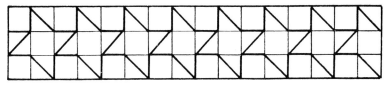

"Stars Around the Nativity" (Fig. 29)

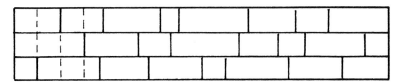

"Plum Blossoms at Nightfall" (Fig. 51)

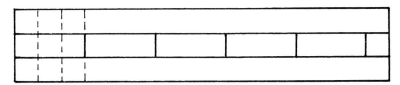

"Alpine Village" (Fig. 1)

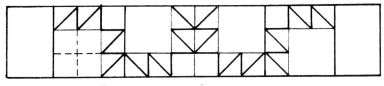

"Tree of Life" (Fig. 44)

Four-Unit Designs

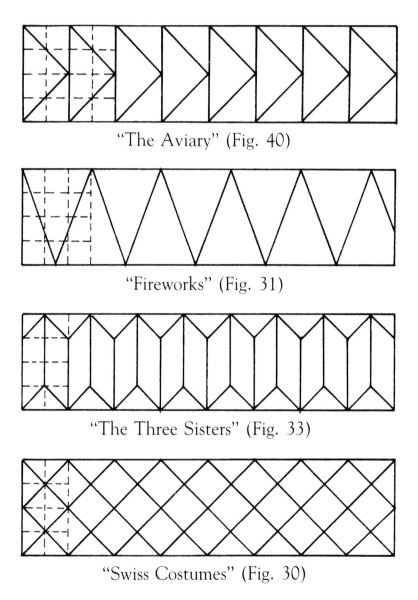

"The Aviary" (Fig. 40)

"Fireworks" (Fig. 31)

"The Three Sisters" (Fig. 33)

"Swiss Costumes" (Fig. 30)

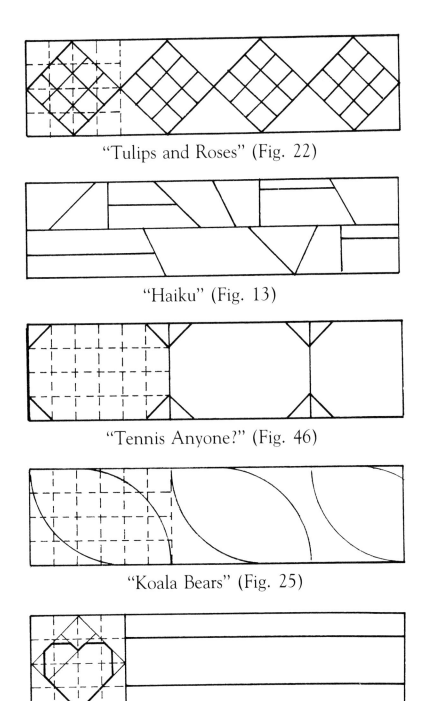

"Tulips and Roses" (Fig. 22)

"Haiku" (Fig. 13)

"Tennis Anyone?" (Fig. 46)

"Koala Bears" (Fig. 25)

"Hand and Hearts" (Fig. 20)

Corners for Borders

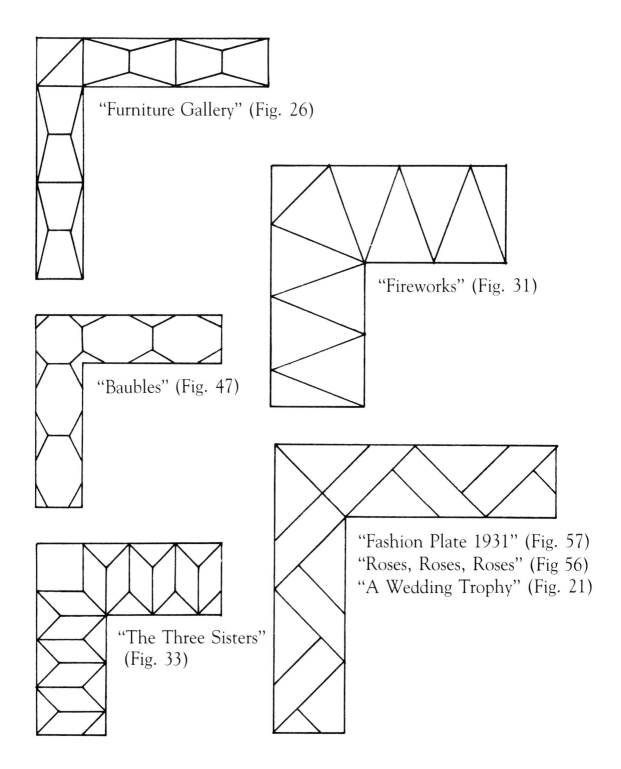

"Furniture Gallery" (Fig. 26)

"Fireworks" (Fig. 31)

"Baubles" (Fig. 47)

"Fashion Plate 1931" (Fig. 57)
"Roses, Roses, Roses" (Fig 56)
"A Wedding Trophy" (Fig. 21)

"The Three Sisters"
(Fig. 33)

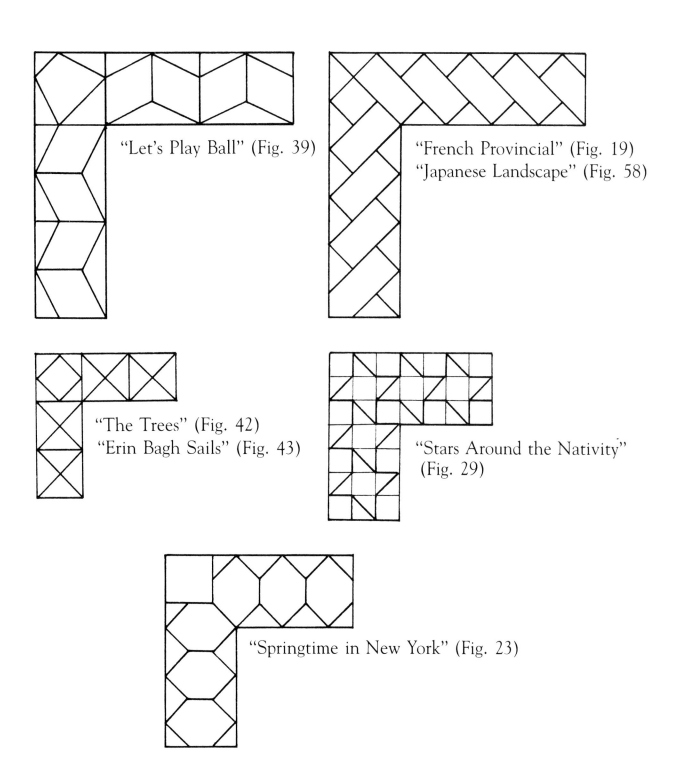

"Let's Play Ball" (Fig. 39)

"French Provincial" (Fig. 19)
"Japanese Landscape" (Fig. 58)

"The Trees" (Fig. 42)
"Erin Bagh Sails" (Fig. 43)

"Stars Around the Nativity"
(Fig. 29)

"Springtime in New York" (Fig. 23)

Block Designs

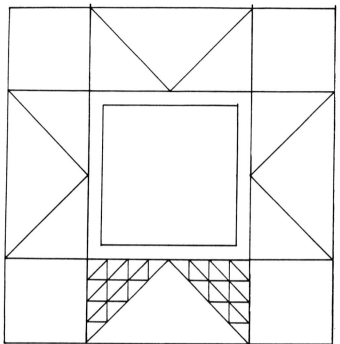

"Swiss Chalet" (Fig. 53)

"Monkey Business" (Fig. 16)
"Scottish Banner" (Fig. 54)

Corner Medallion Sets

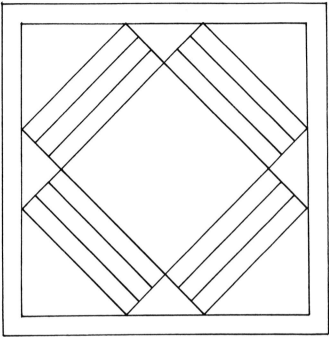

"Sleeping Beauty" (Fig. 17)

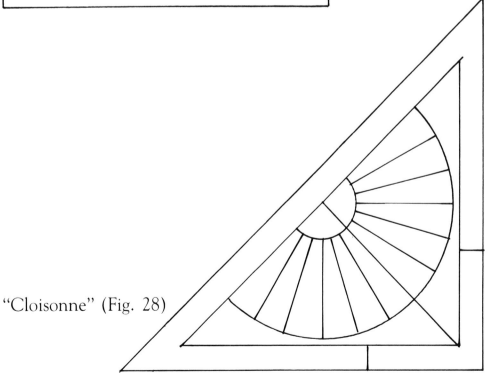

"Cloisonne" (Fig. 28)

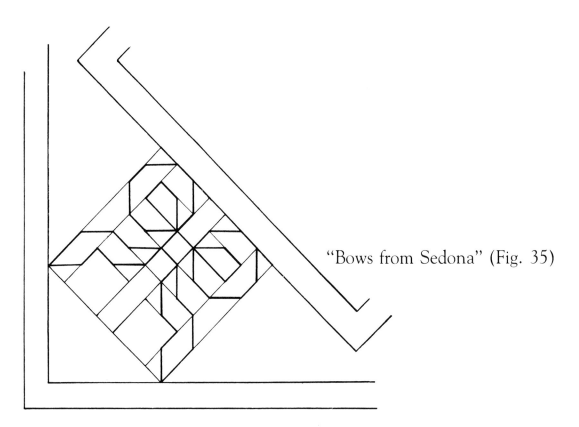

"Bows from Sedona" (Fig. 35)

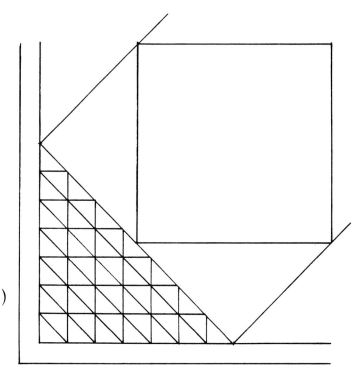

"The Ascent" (Fig. 52)

Asymmetric Designs

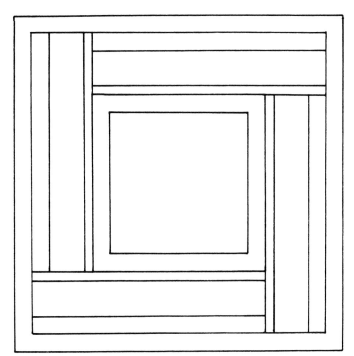

"Dancing Elephant" (Fig. 6)

"Shall We Dance" (Fig. 10)

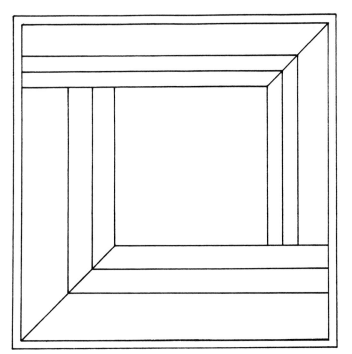

Index to Illustrations

Bibliography

Baseman, Andrew, *The Scarf.* New York: Stewart, Tabori, & Chang, 1989.

Beyer, Jinny, *The Art and Technique of Creating Medallion Quilts.* McLean, Virginia: EPM Publications, Inc., 1982.

Braun-Ronsdorf, Margarete, *The History of the Handkerchief.* Leigh on Sea, England: F. Lewis Publishers Limited, 1967.

Bishop, Robert and Houck, Carter, *All Flags Flying: American Patriotic Quilts as Expressions of Liberty.* New York: E. P. Dutton, 1986.

Brackman, Barbara, *Clues in the Calico.* McLean, Virginia: EPM Publications, 1989.

Christopherson, Katy, *The Political and Campaign Quilt.* Kentucky: The Kentucky Heritage Quilt Society, 1984.

DePauu, Linda Grant and Hunt, Conover. *Remember the Ladies—Women in America 1750-1815.* New York: The Viking Press, 1976.

Higgins, Alice and Lamb, Tom, *Runaway Rhymes.* New York: The P. F. Volland Co., 1931.

Johnson, Bruce, *A Child's Comfort: Baby and Doll Quilts in American Folk Art.* New York: The Museum of American Folk Art, 1977.

McClinton, Katherine Morrison, *Antiques of American Childhood.* New York: Bramhall House, 1970 (MCMLXX).

Meller, Susan and Elffers, Joost, *Textile Designs.* New York: Harry N. Abrams, Inc., 1991.

Montgomery, Florence M., *Printed Textiles, English and American Cottons and Linens 1700-1850.* New York: The Viking Press, 1970.

Musee De L'Impression Sur Etoffes, *Printed Handkerchiefs as Sunday Best and Image of the People.* Mulhouse, France.

Petit, Florence H., *America's Printed and Painted Fabrics.* New York: Hastings House, 1970. Schlotzhauer, Joyce M., *The Curved Two-Patch System.* McLean, Virginia: EPM Publications, Inc., 1982.

Schoeser, Mary, *The London Connection, Number 14: Printed Handkerchiefs.* London: Museum of London, 1988.

Smith, Linda Joan, "None the Worse for Wear", *Country Home* 12 no. 2, pp. 140-146.

Sommer, Elyse, *Textile Collector's Guide.* New York: Monarch, 1978.

Swartz, Elizabeth Moyers, "Collecting Handkerchiefs", *Hobbies,* October, 1973, pp. 105, 126-127.

Weiss, Hillary, *The American Bandana; Culture on Cloth from George Washington to Elvis.* San Francisco: Chronicle Books, 1990.

Weissman, Judith Reiter and Lavitt, Wendy, *Labors of Love: America's Textiles and Needlework, 1650–1930.* New York: Alfred A. Knopf, 1987.